DK

A DK PUBLISHING BOOK

Project Editor Sheila Hanly
Senior Art Editor Rowena Alsey
U.S. Editor B. Alison Weir

Senior Editor Nicola Tuxworth
Managing Editor Jane Yorke
Managing Art Editor Chris Scollen
Production Marguerite Fenn and Catherine Semark

Photography Steve Shott and Susanna Price
Illustrations Robin Jacques and Graham Philpot

Language consultant Professor Elizabeth Goodacre
U.S. Language consultant Professor William E. Nagy
Natural History consultant Steve Parker
Medical consultant Dr. T Kramer
Geography consultant James Mills-Hicks, DK Cartography

First American Edition, 1993
4 6 8 10 9 7 5

Published in the United States by
DK Publishing, Inc., 95 Madison Avenue
New York, New York 10016

Copyright © 1993 Dorling Kindersley Limited, London
Visit us on the World Wide Web at
http://www.dk.com
Photography (page 44 dog, sheep, goats; page 56 camel; page 58 zebra;
page 60 jaguar; page 65 penguin; front cover sheep)
copyright © 1991 Philip Dowell

Library of Congress Cataloging-in-Publication Data

Watson, Carol. 1949 –
    My first encyclopedia / by Carol Watson. – 1st U.S. ed.
      p. cm.
    Includes index.
    Summary: A picture encyclopedia that covers the human body,
the family, homes, pets, sports, and other aspects of the world.
    ISBN 1-56458-214-0
    1. Children's encyclopedias and dictionaries. [1. Encyclopedias
and dictionaries.] I. Title.
AG5.W337   1993
031 – dc20   92-53477
                                                       CIP
                                                       AC

Color reproduction by J. Film Process Singapore Pte., Ltd
Printed and bound in Italy by L.E.G.O., Vicenza

My First Encyclopedia

Carol Watson

Note to parents and teachers

An amazing thing about young children is their fascination with the world around them. While a first encyclopedia cannot be comprehensive, **My First Encyclopedia** has been specially designed to answer many of the questions children ask and introduce them to the exciting world of books – as a source of information about themselves and their world.

A first book of knowledge

My First Encyclopedia is arranged in themes that parallel a child's developing curiosity and interests. Starting with a child's immediate daily experiences, the themes extend to an exploration of the wider world, covering topics such as animals, climatic regions, the people of the world, and even outer space. By reading through the themes in order, you can encourage children to make connections between their own lives and those of people living in other parts of the world.

Looking at pictures

The encyclopedia is packed with stunning full-color photographs that let children see what animals and objects really look like and arouse their interest to know more about them. Detailed drawings show the context in which things are found, and imaginative picture sequences reveal some of the processes that occur both in the natural and the human world. When sharing the book with younger children, you can read the text aloud, using the photographs and drawings as starting points for further discussion. It would be useful to point out to children the conventions of illustration and make sure they understand that not all the objects on the page are shown in scale.

Reading aloud

Many children have stories read aloud to them, but this is not necessarily the case with information books. As a result, beginning readers are often unfamiliar with the written style used in such books and less competent in predicting what the text will "say" – a key step in learning to read. The pages dealing with children's everyday experiences are addressed to the reader, but the more impersonal, instructional style of information books is also introduced. Older children, who are starting to read on their own, will find the clear, simple text easy to follow. The familiar word is always used to name an object or animal, followed by the more specific or technical term. This helps children to read and understand the information easily, and to increase their vocabulary at the same time.

Finding information

My First Encyclopedia is designed to prepare children for more sophisticated information books. A complete alphabetical index is included to simplify the task of locating information on specific topics. You can also encourage children to use the index for cross-referencing. A pronunciation guide for more difficult words has been included with the index. It can be used to help expand children's spoken vocabulary and may also be useful to adults when reading aloud.

A book to grow up with

In sharing and enjoying this book with your children, you will introduce them to an exciting world of information and knowledge that will be invaluable to them throughout their lives.

Elizabeth Goodacre
Language Consultant

Contents

The human body

The human body is made up of different parts, each with a special job to do. All the parts work together so that you can move, breathe, grow, and stay alive.

Skin
Your body is covered all over by layers of skin. The skin protects the inside of your body and stops germs from getting in.

Muscles are attached to your skeleton under your skin. You use your muscles for lifting, carrying, and moving around.

hand

Arms and legs
You lift and carry things with your arms and hands. You use your legs and feet to walk and run.

head

arm

Bones are connected by joints so that people can move and bend.

chest

skull

Inside the body
Inside your body are soft parts, called organs, that do different jobs.

The brain inside your head controls all your thoughts and movements.

elbow joint

hip bone

rib cage

The lungs in your chest breathe in fresh air and take in the oxygen you need to stay alive.

knee joint

The heart is a muscle that pumps blood around your body to give it oxygen and food.

leg

Skeleton
The human skeleton is a frame made of 206 bones. It supports the soft parts of the body.

The stomach is where the food you eat starts to be broken down. Food gives the body energy and helps it grow.

foot

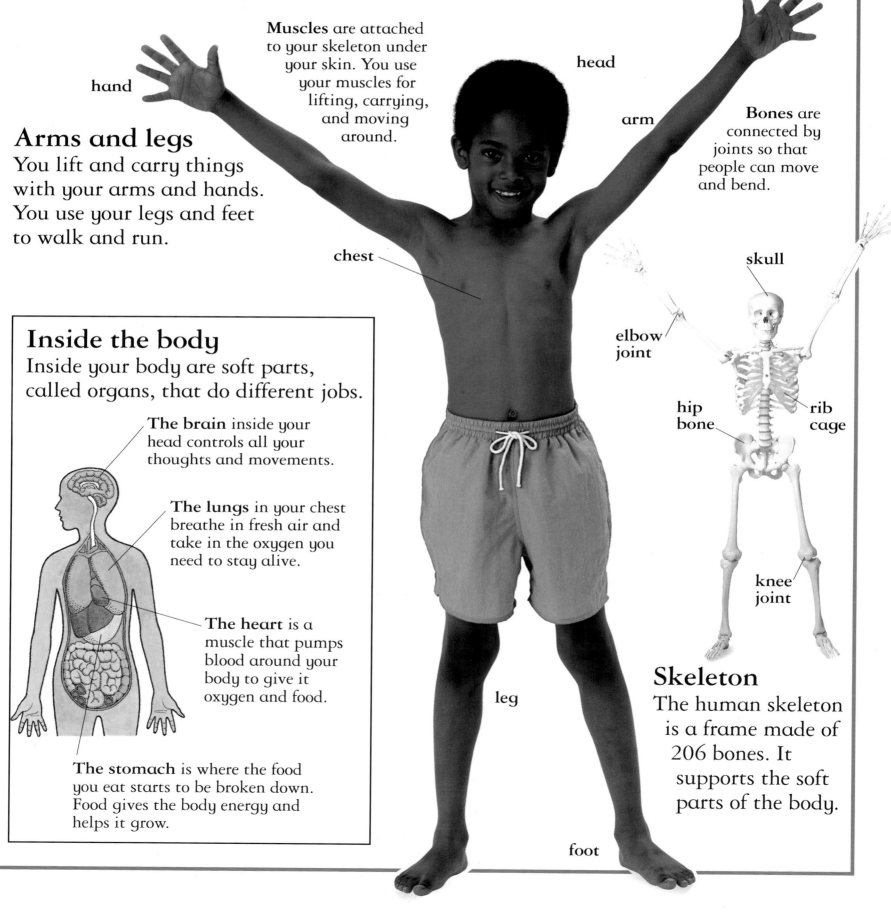

Boys and girls

You are either a boy or a girl. A boy is male and grows up to be a man. A girl is female and grows up to be a woman.

All people look a little different. Not even identical twins have exactly the same face.

Growing up

People grow from the moment their lives begin. As they grow, their bodies change. People usually stop growing when they are about 20 years old, but their bodies do not stop changing.

Speech

The vocal cords in your throat make sounds. With your mouth and tongue, you can shape the sounds into words so that you can speak to other people.

Hearing

You hear with your ears. They collect sounds from the air and send them to your brain. Your brain then tells you what the sounds mean.

Sight

People use their eyes to see. Eyes act like cameras, sending pictures to the brain. Some people need to wear glasses to see clearly.

Taste

Your tongue helps you taste. It is covered with taste buds that can tell if something is sweet or sour, salty or bitter.

Touch

When you touch something, nerves in your skin send messages to your brain. Your brain can tell whether the thing is soft or hard, rough or smooth, hot or cold.

Smell

You smell with your nose. Nerves in your nose send messages to your brain, which tells you what you are smelling.

9

Families

A family is all the people you are related to. Everyone is part of a family, whether it is large or small. Many families get together to celebrate special occasions.

Grandparents

Your grandparents are your mother and father's parents. You are their grandchild.

Some children call their grandmother "Grandma" and their grandfather "Grandpa."

Parents

Your mother and father are your parents. If you are a girl, you are your parents' daughter. If you are a boy, you are your parents' son.

Aunt

If your mother or father has a sister, she is your aunt.

Some children call their mother and father "Mommy" and "Daddy."

Uncle

If your mother or father has a brother, he is your uncle.

Cousin

If your aunt and uncle have children, they are your cousins.

Your aunt's husband is also your uncle.

Sister and brother

If your parents have another child who is a girl, she is your sister. If your parents have another child who is a boy, he is your brother.

These children were born on the same day. They are twins.

A new baby

This family has a new member – a baby girl. Everyone is looking forward to helping take care of her.

A family vacation

Many families enjoy vacations together. This little girl is going to the beach with her father. They will be able to spend lots of time with each other.

Visiting Grandma and Grandpa

A visit to your grandparents can be a special treat. Some children's grandparents live at home with them.

Getting married

When two people get married, they become part of a new family. Both families try to get together to celebrate. Sometimes they wear their best clothes and take photographs to remember the happy day.

Some people have videos made of their wedding so that they can watch and enjoy it all over again.

People often give one another brightly wrapped presents on their birthday.

A birthday

Every year, each of us has a special day – a birthday. Some people have a party on their birthday. They invite their family and friends to share the day with them.

11

Houses and homes

People live in different kinds of homes. Many people live in an apartment or house in one place. Nomads are people who move around, living in tents or vehicles. Some homes are large with lots of rooms with different uses, others are smaller with one or two rooms.

Living room

A living room or family room is a comfortable room where people can read, relax, or watch television.

People may decorate the rooms of their home in the colors they like best.

Trailer home

A trailer home is a house that can move. This large trailer usually stays in one place. Some trailers have wheels and can be towed by a car.

Kitchen

People use a kitchen to store, prepare, and cook their food. Most modern homes have gas or electric stoves for cooking food. Some people eat their meals in the kitchen.

Types of homes

Homes come in lots of different shapes and sizes. Houses and cottages may be built with wood, bricks, or stone. Modern apartments may be made of steel and glass.

On the outskirts of a city, there is usually more space to build individual houses than in the crowded city center.

wooden house

brick house

villa

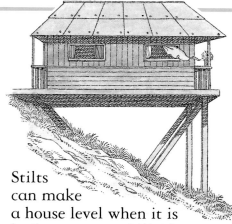

Stilts can make a house level when it is built on a steep hillside.

House on stilts

People who live near rivers and marshes often build their homes on stilts. The stilts keep the house high up off the ground, protecting it from floods.

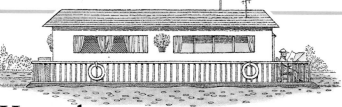

Houseboat

A houseboat is a home that floats on water. Some people live on their houseboats all the time. Others use them as vacation homes.

Bathroom

There is usually a bath or shower, a sink, and a toilet in a bathroom. People use a bathroom for washing, shaving, and brushing their teeth.

Bedroom

A bedroom is a room where people can relax and sleep. People also keep clothes and get dressed in a bedroom. Many children spend time in their bedroom, playing with toys or reading books.

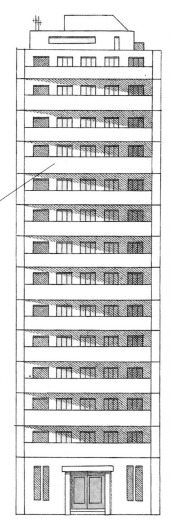

A "high-rise" is made up of many small homes built on top of one another, called apartments. They are built in crowded cities.

apartment building

row houses

high-rise apartment building

Pets

Many people keep tame animals as pets. Pets are fun to play with and care for, but caring for them is hard work. Everyone in the family should agree about getting a pet.

Mouse

A tiny pet mouse should be handled carefully. Mice need a big cage to live in. The cage must be cleaned out two or three times each week.

Pony

Some children are lucky enough to be able to learn to ride a pony. A pony should be groomed and exercised every day.

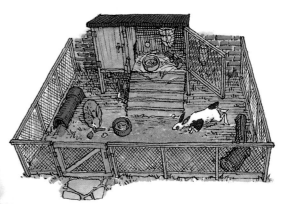

Rabbit

Rabbits are friendly animals. If you play with them often, they quickly become tame. Rabbits need to live in a hutch with a fenced area to hop around in.

Some parakeets learn to copy human voices and say different words.

Fish

Fish are fascinating to watch as they swim around in a big glass tank called an aquarium. These goldfish need to be fed a small amount of food every day.

Parakeet

A parakeet is a small, colorful bird. This chirpy pet likes to live in a large, clean cage — safe from other pets!

Dog

A dog is a good friend and likes lots of love and attention. Dogs need exercise every day to keep them healthy. They enjoy long walks and chasing sticks and balls.

Pet care

All pets need to be kept clean. A dog's coat should be gently brushed to remove loose hair and dirt.

Guinea pig

Guinea pigs are shy animals, but are easy to tame. They like to eat a lot and need plenty of exercise.

Visiting the vet

A sick pet

If your pet is sick, stops eating, or drinks more than usual, it should be taken to the vet for a check-up.

Check-up

The vet will look carefully at your pet for signs of illness and might give it an injection.

Medicine

Your pet may need pills or special food to help it get better. It might have to stay overnight at the vet's.

Cat

Cats enjoy playing and being petted. They also need time alone. After a meal, a cat will spend a long time washing itself carefully. Cats sleep most of the day and wake up to prowl at night.

All in one day

A day starts in the morning, when the sun rises. During the daylight hours, people are busy – working, eating, and playing. By nighttime, when the sun sets, most people are tired and ready to rest.

Morning

In the morning, it is time to wake up, get dressed, and get ready for the day ahead.

Breakfast

Breakfast is the first meal of the day. It gives people energy to keep going all morning.

Off to school

On weekdays, most children go to school. They get to school by walking, riding a bicycle, or traveling in a bus or car.

Time to learn

During the school day, children learn things such as reading, writing, science, and mathematics. They can make friends and learn to work together.

At some schools, children spend time painting and drawing every day. It is a good way to learn about colors, patterns, and shapes.

Teachers help children learn and show them how to find things out for themselves.

Children do different things during the school day. They might spend some time singing and making music together.

Many children enjoy playing ball games in the park.

Afternoon

In the afternoon, when school is over, there is often time to play. Children can play outside or indoors – reading books, drawing, or playing sports.

Mealtime

In the evening, many families share a meal. It can be a time when they tell one another what they have done during the day.

Some families eat their main meal around noon instead of in the evening.

Evening

In the evening, it begins to get dark as the sun goes down. Most people need to rest and relax after a busy day. Some children read a story before bedtime.

Bathtime

It is important to keep your body clean and fresh by washing carefully every day.

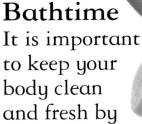

Time for bed

At night, most people are tired. It feels good to go to bed and sleep until morning.

Games and sports

People of all ages enjoy playing games and sports. We play sports for fun and to relax, or for exercise to keep us fit and healthy. Some sports and games are played by people on their own; others are played by many people in groups called teams.

Cycling

Many people enjoy riding a bicycle along country roads with their family or a group of friends. Cycling is good exercise and can be an exciting sport. Cyclists can race one another on cycling tracks.

Ice-skating

Ice skaters wear special boots with a thin blade fixed to the sole of the boot. These help them glide over the ice. People often go to ice rinks to skate on ice that is smooth and safe.

Judo

Judo is a sport for two players. They wear white judo suits and stand on a soft mat. The players learn special movements to throw each other onto the floor.

Swimming

Swimming is a sport that people can enjoy in teams or by themselves. They can race up and down a swimming pool, or have fun splashing and playing with friends.

Gymnastics

A person who does gymnastics is called a gymnast. A gymnast must be strong and supple to jump, turn somersaults, balance, twist, and cartwheel. This gymnast is wearing a stretchy leotard so that she can move easily.

Running

Many people enjoy running in races. They run on roads, on athletics tracks, or across the countryside.

Runners wear special shoes with thick, soft soles to protect and support their feet.

Watching sports

Large sports stadiums are built in many cities. People go to stadiums to watch their favorite sports team in action.

Basketball

Basketball is played by two teams of ten players. Five players from each team work together to score points.
A team scores points when a player throws the ball into the net, or basket.

Wearing a sports outfit, such as shorts and a tank top, helps players keep cool and move freely.

Roller skating

Roller skaters speed along with four wheels attached to special boots or strapped to the soles of their shoes. They wear a helmet and elbow and knee pads to protect them in case they fall.

Ball games

Many sports are played with a ball. Soccer players kick a ball between two goalposts to score points. Tennis players use rackets to hit the ball over a net. Baseball players use a long bat to hit the ball. Football players try to carry the ball across a large field.

soccer ball

tennis ball

baseball

football

19

Keeping healthy

We would all like to be healthy. To help us stay fit and strong, we should try to care for our bodies by keeping clean, eating well, exercising, and getting enough sleep.

Sleeping

Sleeping gives our bodies and minds a chance to rest. Children need more sleep than adults.

Keeping clean

To stay healthy, we need to keep our bodies clean. We should wash all over at least once a day.

washcloth

nailbrush

soap

toothbrush and toothpaste

shampoo

Nails

Dirt collects under fingernails. We should trim them neatly and make sure that they are scrubbed clean.

Teeth

When children are about six or seven, their baby teeth fall out. A new set of teeth grows. We must take care of our teeth properly by brushing them every morning and night, and by not eating too many sweets.

Visiting the dentist

We need to visit the dentist at least twice a year. The dentist checks our teeth and gums to make sure that they are healthy and strong.

If your tooth has a hole in it, the dentist will fill it.

Hair

You can keep your hair clean and shiny by washing it often. Brushing and combing your hair gets rid of tangles.

wasp nest

branch

A logging truck takes the logs to the sawmill.

Timber

Some trees are grown especially for their wood, or timber. When the trees are big enough, they are chopped down. The trunks, or logs, are taken to a sawmill where they are cut into flat strips, called planks.

Tree house

A tree is home to all sorts of creatures. Birds roost and nest in the branches. Squirrels run up and down the tree trunk and make leafy nests. Insects buzz around in the treetops or scurry among the roots.

Bark is the tree's skin. It protects it from insects and diseases.

Wild rabbits live in holes in the ground called warrens or burrows. The entrance to a rabbit warren is often hidden in the roots of a tall tree.

chair

Things made from wood

Many useful things are made from wood. Wooden planks are used for building, or making furniture such as chairs. Wood chips are crushed into pulp to make paper. Fewer trees need to be cut down if old paper is saved and used to make new paper.

plank   wood chips   book

Natural forest

For thousands of years, trees have grown naturally in forests all over the world. Trees are very important because they give off oxygen that all animals, including humans, need to breathe.

Birds

Birds are the only animals that have feathers. All birds have wings, but not all of them can fly. Some birds live together in large groups called flocks, while others live alone.

Breeding

Laying
Female birds lay eggs, often in a nest built high in a tree. The female or male bird sits on the eggs to keep them warm.

Hatching
When a baby bird, or chick, hatches from the egg, its eyes are usually closed. Many chicks have no feathers.

Growing
The male and female birds fly back and forth with food for the chicks. When the chicks' feathers grow, they can fly and feed themselves.

Flight
Most birds have perfect bodies for flying. Their hollow bones are light and very strong. Birds fly by flapping their wings or by gliding on currents of air. Some birds can flap their wings so fast that they hover in the air.

Feather
A bird has different kinds of feathers. Tail and wing feathers help the bird fly. The outer feathers are special colors to hide the bird from its enemies or help the bird show off to its mate. Soft down feathers grow close to the bird's body to keep it warm.

tail feather

body feather

down feather

Kiwi
A kiwi's wings are so small that it cannot fly. It lives and nests on the ground. A kiwi hunts at night. It uses the nostrils at the end of its beak to sniff out food in the dark.

Tuareg people

The Tuareg people of Africa live in goatskin tents in the Sahara desert. They are nomads, moving from place to place to find grass for their camels and goats. Tuareg people use camels to carry their belongings across the desert.

Tuareg people hang their belongings in trees to keep them safe from animals.

Rocky desert

In some deserts the land is rocky and bare. Only plants that store their own water, such as cacti, grow in the dry, rocky deserts of North America.

This rattlesnake buries itself in the sand to keep cool during the very hot days.

Rattlesnake

A rattlesnake gets its name from the rattle on the end of its tail. It shakes its tail from side to side to warn other animals to keep away.

Cactus

A Saguaro cactus grows very slowly. It can live for up to two hundred years and grow taller than a house.

Elf owls nest in holes in the tall cactus plant.

Lizard

This desert lizard has sharp spines on its back. These spines protect it from attack.

Strong, dry winds blow across the desert plains and carve rocks into strange shapes.

Rat

During the day, the kangaroo rat stays in its burrow to keep cool.

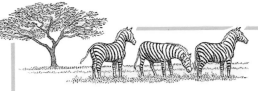

In the grasslands

Zebra
Zebras live in large groups called herds. While the rest of the herd grazes, the leaders watch out for danger.

Grasslands are flat plains where grass, low bushes, and few trees grow. The summers are very hot and dry, while the winters are cold. The grasslands are home to many different animals, from plant-eating elephants and zebras, to meat-eating animals such as lions.

Elephant
An African elephant is the biggest animal that lives on land. The elephant's nose and upper lip form a long, supple trunk. It uses its trunk like a hand to pick plants and put them into its mouth.

An elephant also uses its trunk to squirt water into its mouth.

African savannah
The driest areas of grasslands are called savannah. The African savannah is one of the last places left in the world where there are still large herds of wild animals. Hundreds of animals gather at water holes to drink.

A giraffe's long legs and neck help it reach the leaves at the tops of tall trees.

A hippopotamus keeps cool by lying in a water hole with just its eyes, nose, and ears showing above the surface.

kob

topi

wildebeest

Vulture

A vulture is a bird of prey with very good eyesight. It flies high above the grasslands, searching for dead animals to eat.

Lion

Lions lie in wait at a water hole to pounce on animals that come to drink. They spend the rest of their time asleep in the shade.

Children look after the cattle. They move them around to find fresh grass.

Xhosa people

Many Xhosa people live in villages on the grasslands of southern Africa. They use mud and branches from the plains to build their houses. Living in these barren lands can be difficult. The men often have to leave the family to try to find work in the cities.

Many Xhosa women stay in the villages to look after the crops.

Australian grasslands

Animals such as kangaroos, wallabies, and dingoes live on the hot, dry plains of central Australia. Tall eucalyptus trees grow on the banks of rivers and creeks and are home to flocks of brightly colored birds.

Kangaroo

A kangaroo uses its long tail to balance as it leaps over the ground. A baby kangaroo, called a joey, is carried in a special pouch on its mother's belly.

galah

Emus are the second largest birds in the world. They cannot fly, but they run very fast on flat ground.

Dingoes are a type of wild dog. They hunt together in groups called packs.

In the rain forest

Rain forests grow in hot and rainy parts of the world. Millions of animals live among the thick undergrowth and tall trees. Some live high up in the treetops, where they can see the sun. Here, the leaves and plants make a kind of roof called a canopy.

Tree frog

This tiny frog lives in the forest canopy. It grips the leaves with its sticky fingers and toes.

Canopy plant

This plant grows at the top of tall trees. It lives off rainwater, which collects in its curved leaves.

Hummingbird

A hummingbird beats its wings so fast that they make a humming sound. Hummingbirds hover in the air and sip sweet juice, called nectar, from flowers.

A hummingbird uses its long beak to reach deep inside flowers.

Jaguar

A jaguar is a big wild cat. It can climb trees and swim. The jaguar's spotted coat makes it difficult to see as it stalks through the shady rain forest.

Ants

These ants march along the forest floor. They bite off pieces of leaf to carry back to their nest.

Snake

This snake is called a python. It eats small animals and birds. The python climbs trees by coiling itself around branches.

Monkey

There are many kinds of monkeys living in the rain forest. This monkey uses its arms and tail to swing from branch to branch.

Sloth

A sloth moves very slowly. It spends most of its life hanging upside down in trees. The sloth grips the branches with its long, hooked claws.

Butterfly

This butterfly lives in the canopy of the rain forest. Its colorful wings make it easy to spot as it flies through shafts of sunlight.

Yanomami people

Some Yanomami people still follow a traditional way of life in remote parts of the rain forest in South America. They hunt animals and birds, gather food such as berries and fruit from the forest, and plant crops in small clearings.

A Yanomami man shows a young child how to plant seeds, using a special digging tool.

This baby caiman has large jaws with more than 100 teeth.

Crocodile

Crocodiles, such as this caiman, live near rivers and swamps. They lie in the shallow water, waiting to catch birds and other animals.

61

In the mountains

Mountaintops are bare and rocky and usually covered in snow. The air here is icy cold, so hardly any plants can grow. Animals that can fly or climb, such as eagles and goats, live high up in the mountains. On the lower slopes there are often thick forests, which are home to animals such as bears and wildcats.

Eagle

An eagle is a powerful bird that hunts small animals to eat. Its strong claws, called talons, can grip and carry rabbits, marmots, and squirrels.

Eagles make their nests high up on the mountainside where their eggs will be safe.

Mountaineers wear helmets to protect their heads from falling stones.

Chamois

A chamois is a mountain goat. It has soft pads on its hooves to help it grip as it climbs steep, rocky mountains.

A waterfall can be formed when the snow at the top of a mountain melts and the stream of water drops down a steep rock face.

Mountaineer

Some people climb mountains for sport. They use ropes and picks to help them climb the steep rocks.

Mountain flowers bloom on tiny plants that grow close to the ground. This helps them shelter from the strong winds.

marmot

Wildcat

Wildcats live in the dense forest on some mountain slopes. They prowl at night, hunting small animals to eat. A wildcat's thick fur keeps it warm in the cold mountain air.

Alpine farmers

In mountains called the Alps, in Europe, some people still farm in the same way as they have done for hundreds of years. In the spring, they move their cattle up into the mountains to graze. In winter, the animals are brought back to shelter in the valleys.

Skier

Skiing is a popular sport in the mountains. A skier wears a pair of long, narrow skis to glide over the snowy slopes.

Ski poles have rings on the ends to keep them from sinking into the soft snow.

Skiers wear padded ski suits and thick boots to help them stay dry and warm.

Bear

The huge brown grizzly bear lives in the mountains of Europe, North America, and Asia. It eats almost anything from plants, fruit, and berries to honey, fish, and meat.

Ski lifts or gondolas carry skiers high up the mountainside so they can ski down the smooth ski slopes.

A brown bear's massive legs end in sharp, hooked claws.

In cold lands

The cold lands near the North and South Poles are covered in ice and snow for most of the year. Few animals and even fewer plants can live in these areas. Animals such as polar bears and huskies have thick fur to keep them warm.

Iceberg

An iceberg is a huge piece of ice that floats in the sea. Most of the iceberg lies below the surface of the water.

Polar bear

Polar bears hunt for food on the Arctic snowfields near the North Pole. They catch seals and fish through holes in the ice. Polar bears use their large, sharp claws to catch and kill their prey.

Polar bears have hair on the soles of their feet to help them grip the ice.

Inuit people

Inuit people live in the Arctic regions of North America, Greenland, and Russia. Some Inuit people still live by hunting and fishing as they have done for thousands of years.

Summer days in the Arctic are very long. It is dark for only a few hours.

Seal

This seal lives in the Arctic. It swims fast using its flippers. A thick layer of fat under the seal's skin helps keep it warm in the icy water.

Husky

husky team

A husky is a large dog with a thick, shaggy coat. People who travel near the North Pole use teams of huskies to pull their sleds across the snow.

Life in Antarctica

The only people who live near the South Pole in Antarctica are explorers or scientists. They study the whales, birds, fish, and other animals that live in the area.

Research stations in the Antarctic have powerful radios. The people who work there use the radios to keep in contact with the rest of the world.

Penguin

Penguins live in Antarctica. They cannot fly, but are fast underwater swimmers. They use their short wings as flippers to speed through the water. Penguins spend most of their lives in the ocean, but nest and feed their chicks on land.

Icebreaker ships plow through the frozen seas to open a path for other boats.

Killer whales swim together in groups called pods. They hunt seals, penguins, and squid to eat.

Whale

Many kinds of whales live in the seas around the North and South Poles. A whale swims under the water but comes up to the surface to breathe. It blows stale air out of the blowhole on the top of its head.

65